MEET MY PSYCHIATRIST

by

Les Blacklock

Introduction by Sigurd F. Olson

1977—VOYAGEUR PRESS

To My Parents —
They gave me the freedom to be me.

ACKNOWLEDGMENTS
Portions of ''Meet My Psychiatrist'' and ''Best Seat in the House'' ap-
peared in *National Wildlife*: ''Meet My Psychiatrist,'' October/
November, 1973, and ''Adventures in Moose Watching,'' February/
March, 1968. Reprinted by permission.

Editor: Raymond Bechtle

First published in 1977 by Voyageur Press
    9337 Nesbitt Road, Bloomington, Mn. 55437
Second Printing November 1977
Library of Congress catalog card number: 77-85302
Typesetting, text and binding by North Central Publishing Company,
    St. Paul, Mn.
Color lithography by Bureau of Engraving, Minneapolis, Mn.
Color separations by The Colorhouse, Inc., Minneapolis, Mn.

CONTENTS

INTRODUCTION

When my friend Les Blacklock, a much honored and nationally known photographer of nature, writes a book entitled *MEET MY PSYCHIATRIST*, my shock is almost traumatic. Immediately I had a vision of Les on the proverbial couch having his subconscious probed to find out what Freudian complexes were destroying him.

Being the whimsical, outgoing and delightful person he is, I greeted his idea with considerable skepticism until he explained. The whole concept, he told me, is like sitting on an old mossy log just thinking about nature and beauty and how easily the meaning of life and the hunger of people for communion and wholeness can be satisfied if they only opened their minds; that Nature, after all, is a great Psychiatrist.

I look back over the many years I have known him through work on *THE HIDDEN FOREST*, *THE HIGH WEST*, the famous yearly calendars, countless magazine illustrations, and see an emerging pattern, an intuitive sense of interrelationships and ecological succession, realizing there is a hidden world many never see, a world that could mean the answer to tension and worry.

I will never forget the infinite patience with which he works, waiting for the right light and absolute stillness to catch some flower as it turns with the sun, his deep love of nature and delight in making new discoveries, a sort of pixyish sense of surprise as his magic brings forth some unusual effect.

The magnificent photographs and personal observations in this new book are a testimony to his skill and deep perception, whether of a lace of black ash silhouetted against a sunset or a fluff of snow on a single leaf.

He also sees broad landscapes as with a wide angle lens, not only with his camera but in his mind, catches the meanings of panoramas of the island-dotted Quetico-Superior country or the high fastnesses of the Rockies: alpenglow over snow-capped peaks, mountain valleys shrouded with morning mist. His is an intimate as well as a continental view; but he has not lost in the slightest his first joy in capturing the very essence of any scene and now, as a new departure, his inner feelings as well. *MEET MY PSYCHIATRIST* is a book of unusual dimension, an adventure for the spirit and a delight to the eye.

Sigurd F. Olson

MEET MY PSYCHIATRIST

Tense? Frustrated? Discouraged? Have a tough decision to make? This may be the time to visit my friendly psychiatrist, Old Doc Log. You'll find him patient, willing to listen. And his price is right. His procedures are beautifully simple; the results, impressive.

Occasionally, routine jobs accumulate seemingly beyond our ability to cope with them. Catching up seems impossible. When that happens to me, when I've had it up to *here*, I head for the nearest patch of wild. Doc Log has branch offices wherever there's a rock to sit on, a tree to lean against, waves lapping a shore, a rippling stream. Even a park bench can bring results if there are trees, squirrels, pigeons, ducks — wild, natural things instead of the hard, square lines of man's world.

When I was a student at the University of Minnesota and homesick for my native north woods, my psychiatrist was the bench in front of the whitetail deer habitat group at the Museum of Natural History.

Whenever possible though, I like to visit Old Doc Log himself. He's an old friend as well as my calmer-downer, and a session with him is as enjoyable as it is helpful.

On a recent visit, as I drove up the wild road toward Doc's office, the roar of the engine and the keyed-up tenseness of a long drive kept me from remembering that I would experience *silence* as soon as I stopped and turned off the engine. When I did stop, I was so awed by the quiet that the click of the car-door latch was disturbingly loud.

6

It had been several months since I had been beyond the constant sounds of civilization — freeway traffic, jet planes, power mowers, sirens, air conditioning systems, refrigerators, telephones, TV, people — with never a moment when all were still at one time. Now I could not hear one of those sounds, nor any sound. It was like relaxing music, a symphony of silence.

There is no trail to Doc's office, but it's just off the north edge of a grove of ancient white pines, easy to find.

I walked across the road and stepped into the shallow ditch. A loud WHIRRR stopped me as a ruffed grouse flew from the far side of a thick clump of balsams. I followed its flight by the ticking of its wingtips against branches but failed to get a glimpse of my favorite bird.

"Slow down, Les," I told myself, "and be quiet." Then I started a very slow step/listen/step/look pace. I wanted to *see* the next critter I met.

It worked. A snowshoe hare crouched quietly in its "form" until I was within fifteen feet of it. Then it raised a bit and rocked forward and back, "cranking up" to leap away. I spoke quietly to it, and it froze. I was in mid-stride, so I softly lowered my foot as I talked, waited a bit, then slowly started another step. That was too much. As it jumped off, I whistled softly, and it stopped and sat up on its haunches to see me better. I talked to it for several beautiful minutes while we studied each other. Its nose twitched, and I almost expected a Disney-cartoon voice to answer me.

Under the pines I joined a deer trail and followed it as long as it was going my way. There were many fresh hoofprints in the duff, so I was especially quiet, or tried to be. Heel down slo-o-wly, then ease forward onto the entire foot, trying to compress the needles and unavoidable twiglets so carefully that they wouldn't snap.

"Jay! Jay! Jay!" My presence was announced loudly by a bluejay, so my soft-pedaling stalk then seemed rather silly.

At the north edge of the grove I entered a thicket of head-high greenery. There was a brief flurry from a low cluster of vegetation, and a

7

white-throated sparrow, disturbed and anxious, flitted to a nearby mountain maple. I carefully avoided her nest site and circled around to where Old Doc was waiting.

There he was, larger and more impressive than I had remembered. I stood quietly, admiring the huge moss-covered trunk surrounded by lush ferns and wild flowers.

Old Doc is a model of exemplary living; he took what he needed from the earth, but he has given back much more. For three centuries he stood here, recycling soil, water and air. And even now his life starts to flow into new life — mosses, lichens and fungi. In time his body will be soil, and he will become bunchberry and fern, clintonia and wild rose, birch, balsam, and spruce.

I walked over to Doc, patted his sturdy flank and sat down on his moss-cushioned couch.

I don't really talk to Doc. Not out loud. Our communication is sort of by osmosis. But as I sit there and let it all out, somehow my lesser problems seem pretty inconsequential. Major problems are still major; but as Doc patiently "listens," I can sense what his "answer" is going to be. He waits quietly while I ramble on about a problem that's really been a stickler. Then in the clear silence he allows me unlimited time to mull over the alternatives. It finally dawns on me that it's my move, that Doc is waiting for *my* answer.

Surrounded by the beauty and wisdom of nature, my problem somehow seems less formidable. In this uncluttered bit of time it has been possible to see it alone, in new perspective. My body and brain are refreshed.

I get up.

"Well, Doc, if we're going to lick this thing, I'd better get at it!"

And I do.

FLOOR SHOW

There I was, comfortably seated on a granite boulder, below a broad waterfall, eating supper. The boulder was one of many strewn over a gently sloping granite floor. All had been washed clean when the water was higher and whenever it rained, so my dining room was immaculate.

The river was born in the wilds of the Quetico-Superior country, and the water was clear, soft and drinkable. Because my camp was nearby, I sometimes came to this happy, sunny place to eat.

Summer days are long in the North. I often work with my cameras until quite late and still have plenty of time for supper and a paddle in the canoe before dark.

The lakes with connecting waterfalls and rapids are like strings of beads. It is a wild land of pine, cedar, spruce, birch, balsam and aspen. Moose dunk their heads for water lily roots in the beaver ponds; bears eat themselves fat on sweet berries; and wolves keep deer strong, fast and alert.

Suddenly I was aware of a short-legged little animal coming out of the water onto the sloping rock. It had a small fish in its mouth. A sleek, brown mink, he shook a fine spray on the dry rock, then humped over to where a table-like flat stone was balanced on three others. From my side I could see a small pool of water under the slab roof. The mink vanished under the rock but immediately came out again without his fish, and hopped toward the water. He splashed into the foam and bubbles below the falls

9

and disappeared. I could see his little fish dashing this way and that in the pool.

I quietly ate and waited. There was a fish under there. The mink would be back.

Within minutes the furry fisherman was again ashore with another catch. One fast shake, a quick deposit of the fish under the rock, and back into the foam. Now I could see two little fish in the pool.

Once more he performed the ritual, with one change. He stayed under the protective rock for quite a while. I could see occasional sloshing in the little pool, then it was placid again. When he finally came out, he headed for the roiling water, and I lost him.

He didn't return, so I went down to examine his fish pond. The fish were gone. The mink had a live box! Talk about finicky, gourmet eaters, this critter kept his fish not only fresh but *alive* until the moment he ate them! He apparently liked to eat his supper all at once rather than between fishing trips, and this live box made that possible. Not only was the little pool cool in the shade of the rock slab, but his captive fish were safe from the hungry eyes of gulls and ravens.

THE GIFT

It was a beautiful day in May. Snowfields were melting; migrating birds were singing, hopping, swimming, flying. Spring was waking up all over Yellowstone Park.

And I was in a good place to watch. The Yellowstone River is top waterfowl habitat, a good place for wading birds and shorebirds, songbirds, ospreys, pelicans — you name it. Grizzly bears were up and about. Elk and moose were wading the river.

I was on the west bank, partially hidden by shrubs, but with a good view of the river and of the sage-covered hills rising almost from the water's edge across from me. A sandhill crane was poking among the knee-high sage clumps, catching mice and insects, and probably mixing in a salad of fresh green sprouts. It was like cheating, seeing that very wild bird so close.

I was watching through a remarkable pair of German World War II aerial observation binoculars, ten power, a much appreciated present from Black Hills rancher Francis Murphy. Mounted on a heavy, wooden motion picture tripod, the glasses gave me a clear, rock-steady image. I could watch for hours without eyestrain.

As much as my staring into the private life of the crane may have seemed like window-peeking, I did so with relish.

A movement at the edge of the frame caused me to swing the glasses; and there was a very handsome coyote, still in full winter coat. He

11

too was hunting. He moved quietly among the light gray clumps of sage, stopping now and then to stare at a spot a couple feet away. Then he would do one of three things: ignore the spot and move on; jump and pounce with all four paws on the spot, then lift one paw at a time to see whether he had a vole, mouse or shrew pinned down, in which case he'd eat it; or leap high in the air and come down *mouth first*, with his mouth wide open. After this last antic, he might come up with a black tongue, spitting dirt and utterly disgusted, or with a round, fat pocket gopher in his mouth, *worth* a few mouthfuls of dirt.

After downing two mice and a gopher, the coyote walked down to the edge of the river, lapped a bit of water, then started trotting out a long, flat point which angled into the river down-stream. New grass on the point looked mowed and park-like. I swung the binoculars with him as he moved jauntily along my side of the point, seemingly unconcerned and happy, almost smiling, on this spring day.

But suddenly he drew up and spun around, doing an instantaneous Jekyll-Hyde change. *Now* he was the sneaky coyote of the coyote-roadrunner cartoons — slanty, half-closed eyes, belly to the ground, stealthily stalking back the trail he had just come along.

I moved the glasses ahead of him to see what had caused the turn-around. The river had undercut the stream side of the point, and the sod held an overhang along the edge. Under this overhang was a round ball of fur, a muskrat, at water level.

Along came Mr. Coyote, shadow-quiet, until he was almost above the hidden muskrat. There he stopped. What to do? If he leaped over the edge, shove as he might against air, there just wouldn't be enough purchase to get him back under the overhang, and he'd end up in the drink — probably muskrat-less.

A choice dinner just two feet away! Should he try?

The muskrat's nose twitched. He lifted his head, turned it a bit and sniffed again. Plop! He was gone.

The coyote stood, looked in all directions as if to see whether his fruitless stalk had been witnessed, then trotted off across the point. He *really* didn't want that dumb ol' muskrat anyhow. It was just a practice stalk. But he had gotten within *two feet*!

On the other side of the point a reception committee was waiting: a pair of Canada honkers and a mixed gang of mallards, pintails, green-winged and cinnamon teal. As the coyote approached the bay side of the point, they all swam *toward* him, shouting what I assumed to be taunting remarks. They stopped just beyond a coyote-leap from shore, and *dared* him to catch them.

The coyote surveyed the situation, decided he was being had, and turned to continue his expedition to the end of the point.

But they wouldn't let him off the hook. Like a bunch of teasing kids, they followed right along with him, telling everybody within hearing to watch out, there's a coyote hunting and he's *right here* by us!

The coyote tried to look unperturbed, but you could tell they were getting to him. He'd throw a dirty glance back over his shoulder and twice made a false charge toward the birds. That automatically pushed the pesky bunch out a bit, but it also increased the din that proclaimed coyote presence.

Finally giving up, the coyote trotted back the length of the point and up through the sage to an opening on a bench. Here he got just what he needed — lavish adoration!

As he stood as tall and big and proud as he could, staring straight ahead, a smaller female coyote came romping up to him and fawned all over him shamefully. She rubbed against his legs, his sides, his neck. She reached up and licked his face something awful. And all the time she was wiggling like an angleworm and wagging her tail like a propeller.

Then a strange thing happened. After all that display of affection, he trotted off and she sat down. I followed with the glasses as he switch-backed through the sage to the very top of a high hill. He disappeared over the crest, but for some reason I continued to watch the point where I had last seen him.

Suddenly, against the sky the coyote arched high above the sage and came down mouth first. Soon he came back over the crest and trotted down through all the switchbacks to the opening on the bench. There he came out of the sage with a plump pocket gopher in his mouth, dropped it at his mate's feet, and trotted off — proudly, I presumed.

GALLERY I

I found this young moccasin-flower late one
afternoon on an island in the Quetico-Superior canoe
country. I was so moved by its fresh, graceful beauty
that I paddled back the next morning and spent the
entire day there. As the sun moved across the sky,
the plant was first front-lighted, then side-lighted and
finally back-lighted. Mottled shadows stretched
picture variables almost to infinity.

I head for the nearest patch of wild.

A loud WHIRRR stopped me as a ruffed grouse flew
from the far side of a clump of balsams.

I talked to the snowshoe hare for several beautiful
minutes while we studied each other. Its nose
twitched, and I almost expected a Disney cartoon
voice to answer me.

Under the pines I joined a deer trail and followed it
as long as it was going my way.

If you want to get somewhere, don't follow a
wildlife trail. Moose trails run into bear trails, bear
trails into deer trails, deer trails into fox trails, fox
trails into rabbit trails, rabbit trails into squirrel
trails, and they go up a tree and into a hole.

I'm really turned on by the neat (like Wow!) designs in nature — round, square or triangular stems; parachutes; screws; propellers — that *work*; stickers that cling to you and say, ''Carry me for a while before you plant me elsewhere.'' — like burrs; other stickers that say, ''Leave me alone.'' — like porcupine quills and cactus thorns. There are millions of designs — mostly functional, many decorative, all interesting.

Birds are beautiful to attract a mate. Leaves are on trees to manufacture food; they just happen to be beautiful too. Lucky us! The alternating long and short gills of these fungi hold the caps up very well; the striking design was a big plus for my camera.

Descendants of ancient tree-sized plants, various
horsetails grow in moist woods, in sand or gravel,
even in water several feet deep. Most kids have
pulled them apart and put them back together again
at the ''joints.'' Some are so rich in silica they are
called scouring-rushes.

There he was, larger and more impressive than I had
remembered. I stood quietly, admiring the huge
moss-covered trunk surrounded by lush ferns and
wild flowers.

After the vivid colors are gone, and before the winter snow, it's a good time for hiking. Days are crisp so you can cover miles at a reasonable pace without getting all steamed up. You can see farther into the forest because the leaves have dropped from the understory. Summer visitors have gone home and even most natives tend to stay indoors, so you can have entire forests to yourself. And I, for one, appreciate the rich browns of late fall. Perhaps memories of my hunting days are part of it. If I flush a deer, or even a grouse or woodcock, my heart pounds, and it's a great day.

This black ash swamp is fine tracery at sundown, a
delicate etching two hundred years in the making.

He's called *brush wolf* in the north woods, but he's really a coyote, and he ranges far beyond his traditional prairie home. Welcomed by cattle raisers for controlling rodents, hated by sheep ranchers, the controversial little wolf has gotten lots of folks mad at each other. Persistent poison 1080 (now banned), aimed at the coyote, killed thousands of other animals and birds such as the golden eagle. And that *really* got folks upset! In spite of intensive trapping and poisoning, the coyote has thrived and now roams over most of North America.

I grew up in a land of pine stumps and small aspens;
the 1918 Moose Lake Fire burned a quarter of a
million acres, killed more than four hundred people.
My most-often wish when I was young was for those
stumps to be live trees again.

The terms ''smart as a fox'' and ''foxy'' are well used if they describe someone who can get away with *almost anything*. Fun-loving, mischievous little murderers, foxes make mouse killing seem like delightful, innocent child's play, and chicken killing a real art — if it's happening to someone else's chickens. Swift, graceful animals, foxes can make a large pack of dogs and an army of mounted horsepeople look like fools. Backtracking, running through water and maze-making are among their many tricks. A fox has been known to make almost daily calls at a rural home, teasing the family dog from two hundred feet away, inviting him to come out for a good chase.

I could have photographed a wild rosebud in our yard, but the fact that I found this one near a grand waterfall far up in the Quetico wilderness makes the picture special to me and that beautiful moment indelible in my memory.

BEST SEAT IN THE HOUSE

The show opens every year on September one. And I've been there for enough openings to know that it's always a grand affair — super cast, excellent script, superb staging — the works. In recent years I've had seats front row center in the balcony; *that's* where I want to be every September first!

The theater is Moose Valley, high in the Rockies. The stage is a broad willow flat, with lush grasses, a meandering stream, ox bows and ponds all reflecting bright September blue, some islands of lodgepole pines, and, of course, broad patches of willows. The cast is predominantly bull moose, usually from six to a dozen, with a cow here and there to spice up the story line. Supporting roles are played by a fantastic array of character actors. Some that come to mind from past performances are chipmunks, otters, coyotes, marsh hawks, mule deer, elk and a grizzly bear sow with yearling twins.

My balcony seat is on the edge of a bluff where the stream cuts under a hill. There is enough erosion of the gray sand so the cut stays raw. Each year another few trees topple off the edge as sand drops from around their roots. The bank is so steep that I can look down at a dramatic angle at action in or near the shallow stream where it passes beneath me.

Like all other antlered animals, bull moose grow a new matched set of antlers each year. Starting with the swelling of two soft spots on the bulls' foreheads in May, the new crowns are fully grown by mid August.

33

As the antlers harden, the brown, fuzzy skin or "velvet" that carried blood and calcium to the rapidly growing antlers all summer is no longer needed, so the moose shed this skin by rubbing it off on brush or trees. In Moose Valley many bulls like to use small lodgepole pines as "rubbing trees." Almost precisely as the calendar page is turned from August to September, scattered small pines along the edge of the valley are seen to be freshly ripped bare of bark and branches, with yellow wood exposed on one side of the tree. At the same time, several bull moose are seen with skin hanging in tatters from bloodied antlers.

Within a day or two, some bulls' antlers are completely clean of skin, and if they have used pines as rubbing trees, they may wear *golden* antlers, richly colored by the pitch from the trees. A nearly black, thousand-pound bull moose is a majestic creature as he slowly swings his great head with a massive, many-pointed crown of shining gold.

This is the beginning of the rut, the mating season of the moose. It is time for preliminary "just-for-fun" wrestling matches, bouts that gradually intensify until the rut hits its peak in a few weeks. The rule seems to be that the winners, the finest bulls, should sire the calves to be born the following spring. On the whole this works; many male calves grow to be magnificent bulls, living proof that they were sired by the great champions of an earlier generation. Thus the strength and vigorous health needed to survive extremely severe mountain winters is perpetuated.

It is during this early "training" period that I like to photograph the moose. They are still sleek with summer fat and smooth coats, and their tempers maybe aren't quite as short as they will be later in the rut. Early September can be beautiful in Moose Valley — frosty mornings and pleasant days, or a few-inch snowfall that soon disappears.

My last visit to the valley was rich with memorable moments, such as seeing, for the first time, *three* bull moose in one battle, each hooked to two others, the trio going this way and that, as everybody pushed. Nobody seemed to win or lose, but it sure looked like fun.

I congratulated myself on recording an exclusive event, perhaps the only time it had happened in history, and I had it on film. Jackpot!

Well, that idea was killed in a hurry. Again that day and several more times that fall, I saw triple fights, all with different bulls. It was like thinking you had a one-of-a-kind picture featured on your living room wall, and then discovered the same print in the rumpus rooms of all your friends. It wasn't special at all. Triple matches seemed the norm, at least that fall, and yet I've never seen them any other time or place.

Another day that same fall I was set up on the very edge of the cut, I suspect with some empty space under me, but several bulls were in close, and I wanted to be ready to shoot at any angle. *Any* angle? Not quite!

While I was focusing on bulls across the stream, a slight sound behind me caused me to glance back over my left shoulder, and there, less than ten feet away, stood a marten, ramrod straight, watching me.

I have seen a few martens (one in naturalist Olaus Murie's woodpile) but have never photographed one. So what did I do but watch him, right back, and I appreciated every second of it.

I had no choice. One move and he'd be gone. And even if he had let me slowly turn the camera around on the tripod, I was between him and the camera, and I couldn't focus the telephoto lens that close anyway. I learned long ago, if you can't photograph it, at least enjoy and savor that precious moment.

Cute and cuddly (looking), three pounds of zip wrapped in gorgeous fur, the buff and brown, bushy-tailed little carnivore can scamper through the treetops in relentless pursuit of a red squirrel, and the squirrel is doomed — unless it can find a hole too small for the marten. But even

this super aerialist had better glance behind him occasionally, because the larger, darker fisher can chase *him*
through the trees and catch him.

As I expected, our intense visual contact was brief,
a few seconds of trying to absorb the rare picture of this
handsome creature as permanently in my memory as my
cameras could on film. And then he was gone.

When I turned back to the moose, I was glad I hadn't foolishly
tried to photograph the marten because a bull was entering the stream to
my right and, if it kept coming, would be passing directly under me,
close enough to almost fill my viewer frame. It did keep coming. I
panned with it, composing on the move, and clicked off two shots. Life
can be beautiful!

One morning I was at blufftop bright and early, a fresh roll of film
in the camera, ready to take the best moose fight pictures ever. There
were four bulls visible, well out on the flat. Two smaller bulls were
clacking antlers off to the left, and a dandy pair of heavy-antlered bulls
were shoving, grunting, and churning the soft ground just to the right of
the younger pair. They were far beyond camera range, but an "island" of
lodgepole pines offered cover much closer to the action.

So I slid down the bank, crossed the stream at a shallow riffle, and
started quietly following a moose trail toward the pines, heavy wooden
tripod and camera on my right shoulder. I glanced over at the moose.
They had all stopped fighting and were staring at me.

It was a frosty morning, but I was suddenly flushed with warmth,
and those friendly pines looked very far away. All that separated me from
the moose were thigh-high willows, through which moose can swiftly trot
and man can only flounder.

"Take it easy, Les," I told myself. A steady pace would be least apt to provoke a charge. I glanced again. All four bulls were facing me, a few steps closer, I thought — staring intently, ears cocked forward. I had to watch the trail so I wouldn't stumble on a hummock or step into a hole. I slowly gained on the pines and eventually reached the grove.

Again among "friends," I moved from pine to pine until I was at the edge of the grove closest to the moose. There I set up at the base of a tree, leveled the tripod and looked through the lens. The bulls, now back to their wrestling, were still too far away for good pictures.

Loving my family, I resisted a very weak temptation to go out among the bulls to get my pictures. It seemed wiser at that time and place to wish the moose to come to me. So I wished, wanted and hoped — and it worked.

All four bulls stopped wrestling and started to stroll toward me. No, it was more direct than that. They were coming *at* me. I thought, "*Great*, maybe they'll come close enough to fill the frame with fighting moose," and followed focus as they came closer.

They kept coming.

Finally they were close enough. I waved my arms and shouted at them. "Hey, guys, that's *fine*! Now wrestle some more, and I bet we'll get you published!"

They kept coming.

As they came on, four abreast, I got the uncomfortable feeling they were going to split the difference — two to the right of my tree and two to the left. I glanced up the tree. The first branch was about seven feet above my head. I wondered how fast I could shinny up to that branch.

They kept coming.

Swinging to my left at the last moment, it seemed they were all going to pass by me to one side. So I stayed on the ground. The two biggest bulls were closest. When they were almost opposite me, they stopped.

The nearest bull laid back his ears. That's one sign. The hair rose up along his back and stood deep and bristling on his withers. That's another. Then his big eyes rolled, red-edged, and he rose high, higher, higher on his hind legs, pawing the air with his sharp, black front hoofs, and came CRASHING down with a running charge . . . at the other big bull!

This is an interesting way to make a living.

———————

Fran's elbow between my ribs didn't quite draw blood, but it did wake me immediately (which it was supposed to do) and the only reasons I didn't blurt out a "Yike!" were my deep-set abhorrence of sounds above a whisper in the wilderness and my steel-firm self control. Of course, if I'd been screaming, I couldn't have understood her whispered message that there was a moose fight outside our tent.

I turned up the volume on both ears and lifted to one elbow while I zeroed in on the sounds of clacking antlers and moose grunts. Fran was right. But it just seemed too early in the fall for such activity.

We had been camping on Lake Superior's Isle Royale two months shooting movies, and this *was* the first week in September, but there had been no frost or even cooler-than-summer weather, so there was nothing weather-wise to even hint that it was time for the start of the rut.

I slipped out of our sleeping bag and stood to watch the bulls through a small window at the rear of our G.I. surplus army tent. Fran lifted the bottom of the wall a few inches and peeked out. There they were in the pre-dawn gloom — two black, moose-shaped silhouettes about 150 feet from us, facing *away* from each other, between rounds.

After a brief breather, they wheeled and were at it again, heads down, antlers fitted into a no-slip, mutually protective arrangement so eyes and faces wouldn't be gouged, then shove, snort, push, groan, wheel — each trying to force the other back, parrying for some advantage which their equally matched strength didn't provide. There was an occasional clack of bone-on-bone as antlers shifted when the great beasts wheeled or twisted their swollen necks, but mostly there were heavy sounds — thudding hoofs, straining groans, and angry, volcano-deep bass roars.

They stopped.

They looked directly at the tent.

And they came, running!

We pulled away from the back of the tent where we had been watching because they were right THERE — stomping, shoving, grunting, ROARING, breathing loudly.

We weren't breathing at all! We huddled in mid-tent, trying to sense what was going on through the canvas wall. I didn't actually *see* the tent move in the weak light that came in through the open front, but we both *sensed* that one bull brushed the tent in the struggle. I hastily whispered to Fran that if the tent went down, she should run out onto the old dock, and I'd try to drive them away.

The tent didn't go down, and the stomping and grunting slowly moved on down the shore of Rock Harbor.

Our movie camera was on the tripod all ready for dawn photography. I quickly dressed and quietly followed the fighting bulls along the shore. I would record the battle as soon as my light meter showed some hint of life.

As slowly as the Earth turns, the sky lightened in the east, the sun finally peeked over the wet edge of the world, and a golden streak skipped across the steaming water of Lake Superior. And with those first gold rays and their welcome warmth, *friendship* came to moosedom. The nearly identical bulls lifted their shovel-like racks up among the willows and started peacefully browsing, like two cronies having a sandwich after bowling.

That evening after supper we paddled across Rock Harbor to tell our friends, the commercial fisherman and his wife, about our adventure. They had lived in a log cabin on Isle Royale from April until November for many years. The setting was similar to the fjords of Norway; large drying racks for the fishnets stood beside the cabin. We expected calm reassurance that the moose were only interested in each other, and that we had no worries if we just used a little common sense.

Instead they spent the entire evening telling us of near-death escapes from the sharp hoofs and antlers of mad moose. They told of this fisherman and that who had been treed overnight while the tree-er browsed in the vicinity to keep the tree-ee up there.

They told of two men walking along a trail at night with a lantern and throwing the lantern to one side of the trail and diving to the other to avoid the freight-train charge of a big bull.

They told of a bull pushing his entire head through the wall of a board and tarpaper cabin.

The one that *became* Fran's favorite was the one about the two fishermen who were treed where the largest trees were saplings. The trunks were so weak that they would sway to the ground with the weight of a man. So each man gathered in another nearby tree, and they straddled some very uncertain space ten or twelve feet in the air. The frustrated bull reared and fanned the air between the legs of anxious and nimble fishermen while they danced and swayed to avoid the slashing hoofs.

On and on went the stories.

I steered by compass and flashlight through dense fog as we paddled back across the harbor to camp. The coyotes were howling near our tent, and Fran was very quiet. She had already made up her mind. We were going to move into an abandoned building the next day.

We did move inside and just in time. That very night there were roaring fights and thundering chases through the pitch-black woods all around the building. The walls seemed canvas thin as the frightening sounds echoed through the long building.

––––––––––

We stayed on Isle Royale until mid-November when the last boat took the fishermen to their winter homes in Minnesota. Fran sawed and split wood each day while I was stalking wildlife with the camera, and we enjoyed the *second* warmth of that wood each evening in an old wood stove which worked fine after we cleaned the soot and ashes out of it.

After Labor Day we were the only people on our side of 13 mile-long Rock Harbor. Each week we paddled across to Pete Edisen's dock to meet the *Detroit*, the boat that picked up the boxes of fish from the picturesque remote cabins scattered around the perimeter of the 45 mile-long roadless island. The *Detroit* also brought us groceries and mail and took our orders for the next trip.

It was a romantic way of life, and we enjoyed it all. During the long wintry evenings we read aloud to each other by the light of a kerosene lamp, with our feet on the oven door, entertained by deer mice seeking crumbs in the cracker-box mazes we had built for them. We hated to leave (after an all-too-short four and a half months on the island), but the last boat was the only way home. No one stayed on the island through the winter.

––––––––––

Still intrigued by the moose stories we had heard, I visited many of the Isle Royale fishermen that winter in their North Shore homes and filled a notebook with spine-tingling tales.

41

One of the best, though, wasn't a near brush with death. Ed Holte told me this one.

Ed fished out of Wright's Island in Siskiwit Bay. He and Ingeborg and their family lived there in a charming log home. As with all fishing families with children, Ed and the family dog, Pup, were left alone when school started.

One frosty October morning a sizeable bull moose was strolling through the Holte clearing. Pup bravely announced the bull's presence and stated in strong terms that if he were a little bigger, he'd tear the animal limb from limb!

The bull responded with what Ed decided must be the moose equivalent of a glove slap across the face; he tossed his antlers and did a sort of war dance, kicking the air with first one hoof, then another, both front and rear. Then, having made his challenge, the bull continued through the yard.

It so happened that his route took him directly under the middle of the Holte clothesline, and his antlers were the right height to hook the rope. It stretched taut and snapped like grocery-store string.

Sometimes moose are creatures of habit. The bull showed up in the clearing the next day at approximately the same time, with the same reception from Pup. Again he hooked and broke the clothesline. For several days he did this, with the line getting so knotted and shortened that it would have to be replaced.

"Enough," thought Ed. "I'll fix that bull!"

So each day he replaced the line with thicker rope, and each day the moose seemed to take more pleasure in breaking the rope. Eventually it took considerable effort for the moose to snap the ever-stronger line. Once it broke, however, he'd strut into the forest as if he'd just set a new Olympic record in the clothesline-breaking event.

When the thickest rope had been broken by an awesome, Super-moose effort, Ed played his trump card. He draped a *metal cable* between two supple young trees, so the low point in the sag was at clothesline level.

Ed watched from the cabin window. On schedule the bull arrived, Pup barked, the ritual dance was performed. "Now we'll fix him!" thought Ed.

The moose walked confidently to the cable, accepted it as the clothesline he had to break, carefully fitted his antlers to the metal line, and pushed. The line swung and tightened; the trees started to bend; the bull's eyes rolled and his neck and leg muscles bulged and quivered. The strong young trees flexed so their tops were nearly horizontal; the taut bowstring was not only aiming back, but *up* — and *that's* what did it.

In an explosion of angry frustration the enraged bull charged with thick legs pumping and hoofs churning deep cuts in the earth. His forelegs left the ground, but he was so totally committed to breaking the line that he fought the cable straight up. The fully-drawn bowstring twanged, the bull flipped and came down on his back with an awful WHUMP, flopped onto his side, and lay there dead.

Well, not quite. But for a while there, Ed thought he'd killed a moose and wished he hadn't gone quite that far.

The stunned bull eventually started to breathe again, raised slowly and unsteadily to his feet, and staggered off through the forest.

DOING WHAT BEAVERS DO

Now there's a *smart* animal. That's what many people think when they see a substantial beaver castle with a moat around it.

I can prick that bubble. At least in one instance. I found where one beaver, in fixing a dam after a winter of necessary neglect, used chunks of inch-thick ice along with sticks and mud to patch his dam.

O.K. So that beaver didn't reason that ice melts. That's one example of beaver creativity gone wrong, but I'll have to admit that, by and large, inherited beaver wisdom, instinct, doing what beavers do, works very well. And what beavers do fits into the whole of nature and the Big Plan very well.

We all know what beavers do; they cut trees, build dams, build houses, dig canals.

But here's what else happens:

The dams create ponds and—

Ducks nest and raise their young on beaver ponds.

Herons hunt frogs, crayfish and small fish in beaver ponds.

Moose and deer cool off, escape insects, browse and graze in beaver ponds.

Muskrats build reed houses which make nest platforms for ducks in beaver ponds.

If a stream dries up in a rainless period, wildlife can still find water in the ponds.

Beavers are the original flood control engineers. Their dams slow the flow of heavy rains and spring runoff which, coming from many streams, would add up to floods downstream. Some of the pond water seeps to underground supplies, helping to keep water tables high.

Beavers tend to "log off" one grove of aspens at a time, and hundreds of new young aspens shoot up from the still very much alive root systems, providing browse for deer as well as the very best habitat for ruffed grouse.

When a pond is vacated after the current crop of aspens has been logged as far back from the pond as beavers dare venture, the untended dam washes out, leaving the muddy bottom exposed. The beaver "meadow" grows grasses and flowers and may stay meadow-like until a new pair of beavers moves in in fifteen or twenty years when surrounding aspens are again ripe for cutting. The meadow is a very different habitat from the forest and will support many kinds of plants and wildlife. For instance, it is a dandy place for foxes and coyotes to hunt for the mice that find grass seeds and grassy cover in the meadow.

I canoed up a small stream in Ontario's Quetico Provincial Park one evening near sunset, hoping to see a beaver, or even a moose. Sure enough, around the first bend, a very large beaver, as much as eighty pounds perhaps, swam slowly ahead of me. Around each bend there he'd be again, just keeping a comfortable distance ahead.

Around the last bend there was a five-foot-high dam, dead ahead. He'd have to expose himself now. The fat slowpoke had no choice but to waddle up over the dam while I drifted in close for a good look at a really big beaver.

Oh, yeah? Suddenly there was a tidal wave coming down the stream toward me with Mr. Beaver under it. There wasn't room for him to pass on either side of the canoe, and the stream was just inches deep. Where would he go?

I was already on my knees, which is the way I usually paddle when alone, so I placed the paddle across the gunwales, raised up so I'd be ready to lean either way fast, grabbed a thwart and hung on.

The big wave kept rolling toward me, and it actually had a foaming crest in the middle. There was no obvious place to go, but he kept coming, straight at the canoe. I spread my knees, gripped the thwart with arms well apart, and braced for the whump that was going to happen.

But it didn't. Up went the bow, and up went the stern with me in it, then down again. No bump, no sound; just a quick roller coaster ride! He had lifted about six feet of stream, the canoe, a big rock I put up front to weigh the bow down when I'm alone, and me; WOW!

I looked behind me and watched the wave swoosh around the bend.

GALLERY II

If you think wildlife photography is demanding, try shooting vegetation. Would the leaves stop bobbing before the snow melted? Obviously they did, but it was touch and go.

The Lilliputian world of lichens and mosses can be gauged by the brown pine needles. I found these red-capped British Soldiers lichens and tiny moss ''palm trees'' in a crack in the granite of the great Canadian Shield. It was a cold, wet day in September, but they seemed all the brighter for it.

When I pinch white cedar, I smell Christmas.

My last visit to the valley was rich with memorable moments such as seeing, for the first time, *three* bull moose in one battle, each hooked to two others, the trio going this way and that, as everybody pushed. Nobody seemed to win or lose, but it sure looked like fun.

"If I were you, Mister, I'd scramble up a tree real fast." On this occasion I thought it wise to do that, and stayed up there until this touchy bull moose left.

The bull did keep coming. I panned with it,
composing on the move, and clicked off two shots.

This is what our "lawn" looks like now. When we moved to a northern hardwood forest, we sold our lawn mower and have encouraged native plants to re-cover the disturbed ground. Now we rake leaves in the woods and put them *on* the yard. Hepaticas are among our earliest spring flowers.

Did the beaver make the tree fall that way? Nope. A beaver chews around a tree until it topples, and he has to be careful to keep from being clobbered.

Now there's a *smart* animal. That's what many people think when they see a substantial beaver castle with a moat around it.

In rich soil under a hardwood canopy, the large-flowered trillium exuberantly heralds spring. In a flagrant exhibition of shameless lily-gilding, the show-offs finish their spring extravaganza with a delicate pink blush.

Black ducks are dabblers. And dabble they do —
along shores, in shallow rapids, in maze waterways
through beds of wild rice.

The Grand Teton Cathedral Group belongs to us all,
and I am thankful.

Most of us are apt to think of great rock domes and cliffs, of high waterfalls and giant conifers when we remember Yosemite Valley. But many times, in searching for foreground frames, I've been drawn to white oaks, and often I feature that handsome tree, allowing the great cliffs to be nice blues in the background.

THE PHANTOM BUCK

They had him now. Circled in. Brush waist high. Each man could see those on either side of him. The huge old "swamp buck's" tracks were being followed going into the circled area, and there were none coming out. They had him!

Elmer Westholm told me about it. Almost every member of the logging crew (of which he was one) had glimpsed this legendary giant at least once, but never with rifle in hand. Deer hang around logging camps to browse each night on branches of felled trees. And loggers often see them as they return to work in the morning.

But this buck was an apparition, a ghost, a phantom. His huge tracks were everywhere, yet none of the crew had ever had a really *good* look at him, just a quick glimpse as he was disappearing into the forest. But that was enough to know that he was the grandad of 'em all, and every logger dreamed of the moment he would see that great, dark beast across the sights of his .30-.30.

And now they had him — in a cut-over opening of stumps, grass and belt-high brush, three inches of last night's snow, minutes-old tracks. Each hunter, rifle high, barrel up, was ready to draw down on the buck as soon as he cleared the circle.

The noose tightened. And so did nerves. Ever so slowly, one step at a time. Everybody could see everybody now.

The circle was as small as the mess hall. How long could he hold?

Easy — easy. Careful. Don't shoot crazy. No deer is worth any-body gettin' hurt. Thirty feet across. Twenty-five, twenty. *No deer*!

The buck had slid on his belly between two hunters and escaped — probably in the last couple of minutes, because his tracks led to the very center of the circle.

I'm always glad to see a famous buck, ram, bull or muskie get away. His legendary size or antler or horn measurements could probably never be matched by the real thing. Besides, once you've nailed him, the fun is over; the speculative record measurements have shrunk to realistic mediocrity. And next year's hunting or fishing season is not the exciting prospect it would have been had The Phantom Buck still been out there.

NO ROAD TO MENOGYN

We were sort of crossing West Bearskin Lake together. I was on snowshoes on the trail from the landing on the south shore to the camp on the north shore. The doe and twin fawns were on a parallel deer trail crossing the lake farther east.

I was doing the winter part of a summer-winter naturalist's evaluation of the Minneapolis YMCA Camp Menogyn, the staging area for "Y" canoe, snowshoe and ski trips in the Minnesota-Ontario border wilderness. A group had been up for a weekend, but had left. I had Menogyn, and the wilderness, to myself.

The nearly mountainous lake and forest area around Menogyn is timber wolf country, a true wilderness of virgin white and red pines, white cedars and white spruce, of deep lakes, tall granite cliffs and steeply rolling hills. In my summer explorations I had found a huge white pine that was eleven feet seven and one-half inches in circumference breast high and had written that into my study as a challenge to campers. With map and compass, *try* to find one larger.

There are occasional openings in the forest where a big pine, spruce or balsam has fallen. Here sunlight can nourish mountain maple and red-osier dogwood — good deer browse. The deer are, of course, prime dinner targets for the wolves. These wolves are the last, the *only* remaining viable population in the lower forty-eight states.

The deer probably accepted me as a distant "companion" on our hike over the ice because humans cross quite frequently on the lake trail. There is no road to Menogyn.

Suddenly the doe stopped, stared hard at the north shore, made a high leaping turn, and ran back toward the south shore. The fawns followed her bobbing flag and, as is the way with whitetails, bobbed their own.

I, of course, looked northeast for the reason but saw nothing.

Yes! There *was* something. A dark figure, black against the snow, moved out from behind a point; then came a second figure, and a third. They were against another far timbered point, so I couldn't see clear silhouettes. More figures came — four . . . five . . . six . . . seven, all evenly spaced and, so far as I could tell, all in the trail of the leader.

The deer were back in the forest now, but the line of figures kept coming. I stood motionless. They would come much closer if they joined the deer trail.

They moved steadily toward the end of the point. Soon I would see them clearly against the snow and, if they kept coming my way, get my best look ever at one of the rarest sights anyone can see — a pack of eastern timber wolves in clear view crossing a half mile of snow-covered ice. My heart pounded. Electricity went up my backbone.

Now, almost to the end of the point.

THERE!

Hey! They're *vertical*!

Skiers! Cross-country skiers!

NUTS!

The skiers curved down toward the far end of the lake. There's a small resort down there that obviously catered to some winter business.

The deer started across again. And so did I, a bit deflated, but still flushed by the excitement of what I *thought* I had seen.

Nearing camp, I left the trail and went into the bay west of camp to the Daniels Lake portage. Partway across the portage I found what I was after, wolf tracks — fresh ones. A single wolf had crossed the portage trail heading west. I carried compass, map and lunch, and was prepared to follow the wolf most of the day hopefully to find a wolf-deer encounter written in the snow.

The track led up out of the Daniels portage valley and curved to the southwest. It dipped down into a black spruce-tamarack bog and crossed the slow, beaver-dammed stream that flowed from a lovely little lake into West Bearskin. That beautiful lake was called Stooey-Dooey by the campers.

We — the wolf and I — wound through more spruce-tamarack bog beyond the stream. Sometimes the wolf tracks were on top of deer tracks; sometimes deer tracks, on wolf tracks. Then we started up a long rise to the west. There were windfalls that the wolf went under and I had to snowshoe around, but keeping to the lone, fresh track was easy.

Now he seemed to be in an old wolf trail with no other tracks but his. There had been at least two snows since the trail had last been used.

Just over the crest of a rise, the wolf had leaped off to the right. This was it! I followed the plunging leaps that were five feet apart.

Just twenty-five feet off the wolf trail, two deer had been eating old man's beard lichens from the dead lower branches of a balsam. The deer had been facing west, the same direction the wolf was traveling, so he had come up the rise to their left rear and was almost opposite them when he had seen them and immediately charged. They had reacted at once, turned and leaped at the same time. The wolf's lunges curved to intercept their flight.

The difference was immediately obvious. Each leap of the deer carried them twelve to fifteen feet; each leap of the wolf five. I pushed my metal tape down through the fluffy snow. Twenty-eight inches with no resistance. The wolf's big paws could get very little purchase in the givey stuff.

But the deer's sharp hoofs had cut right to the hard ground, and with each leap they had soared high and away, with snow flying and graceful bodies arching in that famous escape so often painted by wildlife artists. Wouldn't that have been great to see?

I followed one deer that had veered off to the northeast. Within 150 feet it had slowed to short plunges. Within 200 feet it had begun to browse. The other deer showed a similar pattern to the southeast. There had been very little energy expended by either deer.

The wolf, of course, made a small circle, perhaps only twenty-five feet across, and rejoined his trail heading west.

That's the whole story. The test had been made, and both deer were healthy. There was absolutely no chance of catching them, and both wolf and deer knew it. I could see lots of hungry wolves under those conditions.

Perhaps many tests have to be made before catchable deer can be found. *No wonder* wolves feast on fifteen or so pounds of meat when they make a kill. The next meal might be a long time ahead.

GALLERY III

Son Craig was still asleep in the tent the first
morning out on a 16-day canoe trip. I was under a
black cloth focusing on this image upside down on a
ground glass, trying to do everything right, but *fast*,
before the summer sun "burned off" the early
morning fog.

I should have shared the sunrise with Craig; but if
I'd taken the time to wake him, I'd have missed this
shot. I seemed all thumbs as it was, fumbling my
sleep away, trying to level the tripod, compose,
focus and expose correctly. Why didn't I call to
Craig to wake up? Could *you* have in that setting?
It'd be like shouting in church. I pulled the slide,
released the shutter, double-checked. Had it!

I was being watched. A periscope was out there,
aimed at me. It was an otter, of course, wanting to
play games. Now I woke Craig, and away we went,
paddling out to play hide-and-seek with a
streamlined imp.

Sometimes, although rarely, humankind builds
structures that blend, rather than clash, with nature.
Naturalist-author Sigurd F. Olson's "Listening
Point" is one of these. Many New England farms fit
beautifully into their valleys, complementing both
forest and stream. Lake Superior fish houses, such as
this one, certainly belong in this select group.

Man has had effect on every square foot of land on earth. And yet man is no more master over "his" land than the next rain allows him to be.

A great gray owl is dead wood — a dead stub on a
branch, the top part of a gray stump. There it sits,
being dead wood until prey is sensed below. Then
. . . a turn of the head to focus eyes and ears, a
slight lean forward, a controlled drop. Supper.

Alaska: snow, ice, glaciers, tundra. Of course. But also thousands of square miles of forest. Much of interior Alaska's forest is stunted and slow growing; but when I drove down the Haines Highway toward the southeast panhandle, I found taller forests near the coast. Here black cottonwoods are on the floodplain floor of the Chilkat River Valley. The lower slopes of the coastline mountain ranges support a rich mixture of evergreens: Sitka spruce, Alaska cedar, western and mountain hemlock, and lodgepole pine.

Dainty nibblers, a doe and a fawn are, to most of us,
symbols of gentleness, peace and beauty. Yet mule
deer are also among the toughest of western wildlife.
At home in arid deserts or among snow-capped
peaks, these handsome creatures are obviously doing
fine on this sunny February day. But they also must
survive howling blizzards and long, subzero winter
nights.

A pen, a cob, and two cygnets. Those terms, unfamiliar to most of us, tell us that we are looking at a female, a male, and two young of the trumpeter swan. Fittingly, they are on the shore of Swan Lake, ice-fringed on this late September morning in Yellowstone National Park. Never really abundant like their cousins, the whistling swans, the trumpeters teetered on the edge of extinction until protected by tough laws and the establishment of refuges for their benefit, especially the Red Rock Lakes Refuge in Montana. These healthy cygnets should be able to fly with their parents to lower elevations before freeze-up.

Can you imagine water looking more refreshingly drinkable than this? Not far below timberline, this Montana stream is still close enough to its snow field to be just as cold and pure as it looks.

Almost every fall there is *one day* that surpasses all others. The air is softer, the leaves are at their brightest just before they drop, and the temperature is just right. This was such a day in upper New York.

Because his high-altitude mountain home is snow-covered most of the year, the hoary marmot spends the bulk of his life in hibernation. When he is up and about, he dines well in the lush alpine meadows, growing fat for next winter's "sleep," and suns on the rocks, recouping some vitamin D lost during the long darkness underground.

But when a golden eagle flies over, you'd swear the marmot's fat is all air. He flattens like a punctured tire, trying to blend into the rock so he throws no shadow. If the eagle really threatens, though, he can scurry under his rock home in a hurry.

Without spines, cactus would be eaten. However,
visually I can feast by the hour without being stuck.

Is there a more cheerful bouquet on the spring
landscape than marsh marigolds? Whether the day is
bluebird weather or stormy, marigolds glow as
brightly. Large wetlands can contain acres of marsh
marigolds, but even wholesale abundance can't
diminish the specialness of these fresh beauties
because they will all be gone soon, until next spring.

ONE HOT AFTERNOON IN JULY

The news each day seems to weigh heavily toward human error in the way we live on Earth. We goof a lot.

We look to science for magical answers to all of our physical problems, and we are still frustrated.

Maybe we should look not to man but to nature for a way to go. I suggest a *tree* sets a good example of how to live.

"A tree! A TREE?" you say. "What can I learn from a tree? It's nice to have in my yard, but it doesn't *know* anything. It's just there."

Now wait a minute. Trees have been on earth almost *forever* (compared to man). That's a lot of evolution, a lot of trial and error, a lot of learning how to live. The fact that they're still here is proof that they're doing something right.

Just look at what a tree does. All through its long life it helps us breathe, taking carbon dioxide from the air, giving oxygen back. Its fallen leaves form soil beneath it, from which it and other plants grow. Perfect recycling.

Birds nest in the protection of its branches.

It provides seeds, nuts or fruits — food for wildlife and man.

As branches are broken by snow, ice or wind, they rot back into the trunk or thick branches, making holes for wood ducks, hooded mergansers, goldeneyes, owls, raccoons and squirrels. Woodpeckers chop into the maturing trunk, providing homes for themselves, chickadees, and other small birds.

A fox den under the roots may be used off and on through the years by foxes, woodchucks and other denning animals.

The tree, with surrounding trees, forms a forest, providing protection from storms in winter and cool shade in summer. The forest is habitat for many kinds of birds, animals, shrubs, grasses and flowers.

If the tree becomes really old, its crown will stand above the surrounding forest and may be used as a nest site for many years by a pair of red-tailed hawks.

It is a hot afternoon in July. Thunderheads pile high in the west, building, building. Whipped-cream white on top, the storm is dirty gray on its underside, and ominously yellow-gray green in its boiling midsection. An audible threat is the almost continuous rumble from within.

In a small village directly in its path, townsfolk gather in small groups in their front yards, looking up at the awesome sight. All are quiet, wide-eyed, alert. So far, not a breath of air movement.

One woman, suddenly remembering, hurries to her backyard to remove a few things from her clothesline.

Pink flashes blush in repetitive sequences deep in the folds of the mass. The storm grows frighteningly fast as the churning clouds keep boiling up and out. Now sharp-edged thunder follows each sequence of flashes.

Finally the creamy top hides the sun. The opaqueness of the clouds is felt at once as solid shade quickly drops the temperature a few degrees. The first air movement rustles a few leaves, then hesitates.

The menacing rumbles grow louder.

The edge of the wind, the front, a tight, horizontal rolling cloud almost white against the dark blue-gray base of the storm above and behind it, has been flying low, sneaking up on the town hidden by a forested hill. Now, just before it strikes, the people can see it coming over the treetops. They scurry onto porches or into their homes.

There are thumps of slamming windows around the town. A car races down a street; the hardware store owner has remembered that his wife is out, so he scoots home to shut up the house.

The topmost leaves of the tree move a bit, stop, flutter again. This is the calm before the storm, as if the monster is taking a deep breath, creating a huge vacuum soon to be filled with explosive force. Then come the first hesitant puffs and a spattering of large raindrops. Treetops to the west start bobbing. There is a rushing sound and rivers of wind start to flow in many crazy directions over the top of the forest. The large raindrops are still scattered.

SPLASH! Like a bucket of water in one's face, the rain comes in a horizontal deluge. It is dark at once; lights go on in town.

Trees are like grass, swaying in arcs so broad it's a wonder any

91

can stand. All is silhouette now, bent trunks with dancing crowns, black against the blue-white flashes. Rifle cracks of lightning come often; the rumble is continuous. Wiggly white streaks connect sky and ground. The wind is a rushing roar.

Under the tree is a loud snap. A major root has broken. More roots let go in the onslaught of the wind. Like the climax of a Beethoven symphony with thunderous tympani and clashing cymbals, the mighty tree gives way. Branches are torn from its trunk and from neighboring trees as it crashes to the ground amid the wild roar of the storm.

Settling quickly to a slanting downpour, the heavy rain tries to wash gullies in the forest soil; but twigs and leaves quickly form little dams, and the soil holds.

The rain is soon over, and the storm passes to the east. There its full glory is lighted by warm, late sun. Boiling and billowing to tremendous heights, the great storm is again admired by people in the town. Some have walked to the lakeshore to see it better, and are rewarded with double beauty as the now calm lake mirrors the grand scene.

The following day is as blue-skied as a day can be. All colors are intense in the freshly washed world. Wet leaves still drip in the morning cool.

The forest has seen hundreds of days like this — scrubbed, sparkling days following a cleansing storm.

But this storm has created a change. A great tree has fallen. And a dramatic, long-lasting sequence of events is about to take place, starting *now*.

The big opening in the forest ceiling lets morning light into the understory. The warm sun quickly dries the vegetation. As the sun climbs higher, a broad patch of intense sunlight bathes the forest floor with life-giving rays for the first time in over two hundred years. The deep leaf-mold soil is ready. Moistened by yesterday's inch or more of rain, laced with thousands of seeds planted here by nature's ingenious ways, this garden is ready to burst forth with life unknown on this ground for two centuries.

Shrubs and flowers will spring up; and berries, nuts, grasses. There will be browse for deer and rabbits, cover for grouse and small mammals, nesting sites for birds that prefer the new habitat. Chipmunks and white-footed mice will pull the grass stalks down with their little hands to get at the nutritious seeds.

And what about the dead tree? Dead, my eye! That great trunk is still *full* of life. Man invented death. Nature knows only continuing life, passing from form to form, beautifully, forever.

The handsome log will be that — a handsome log, for many years. And it will continue to serve the forest in many ways.

When the tree fell, the upturned roots exposed yards of mineral soil. Grouse will soon discover this fine source of grit. They and smaller birds will take dust baths here. Tree seeds that need mineral soil to "catch" may start in this bed.

The thick trunk is hollow near the base, as are some of the bigger branches. A bear might winter in the trunk; raccoons, chipmunks and other mammals may den in the branches.

Insects will start at once to break down the wood into soil. They'll work on the inside while mosses, lichens and fungi will start the transition process from the outside. Before long, the entire log will be a lovely green velvet moss garden, enhanced by colorful lichens and toadstools. Still surging with life, the log will enrich growth here for decades.

Source of oxygen, air purifier, provider of food and cover, home for wildlife, soil builder, a beautiful part of the natural world — the tree is an exemplary citizen.

I think you'll agree that the world is a better place because the tree was here.

GALLERY IV

The tree.

The rain is soon over, and the storm passes to the
east. There its full glory is lighted by warm, late
sun. Boiling and billowing to tremendous height, the
great storm is again admired by the people of the
town.

"Isn't it a nice day?" usually means clear and warm
(even *hot*) with perhaps a few billowy clouds and a
whisper of a breeze. But I'm apt to say, "Isn't it a
nice day?" during a thunderstorm, or when it's
thirty-six below. This rainy morning in
Washington's Cascade Mountains was a *very* nice
day.

As snowfields melt back, glacier lilies emerge by the millions, obviously the only plant in these Glacier Park alpine meadows. NOT SO! Soon the yellow mass will be replaced by the bobbing heads of Coulter's daisies; and they, in turn, by a splendid garden of paintbrushes, gentians, shooting stars, swamp laurel and many more mountain flowers, all on this same ground.

Mount Rainier is always GREAT — its awesome
size, its massive glaciers, its many moods in cloud
cover. But Rainier in early October is something
else. The huckleberries and mountain ash put colors
on her flanks that bring spontaneous AHHHHs from
confirmed stoics.

Many a wilderness visitor has heard the midnight
howl of the timber wolf and gone back to the city
thrilled by that memory. It would be a shame to spoil
that illusion, so I won't tell 'em they were hearing
the "lonesome" call of a loon if you don't. O.K.?

The loon is a goose-sized diver, catching fish
sometimes a hundred feet or more beneath the
surface. It is a fast flier but seems overloaded in
flight. It "runs" on the water a great distance before
being airborne and then may have to circle to gain
altitude to clear surrounding trees. The landing is
like that of an airliner, gliding just over the surface,
touching down gently, then surfboarding before
settling in.

If you come *one step* closer, just ONE STEP, I'll
scoot to the very top of this tree!

The background music for this last moment of
sunglow at Dead Horse Point, Utah, was superbly
tasteful — absolute silence. Such *vast* silence —
endless canyons rim full of it — impressed me more,
in this setting, than any sound could have.

Sometimes the green herons created Oriental art
along our shore in Eden Prairie.

For twenty-three exciting years Fran and I lived on this wild bay in suburban Eden Prairie, Minnesota with deer, fox, egrets, owls — a long list of wildlife. Son Craig grew up here. The Eden Prairie land is becoming surrounded by city, but is being preserved as part of a large land-and-water nature center.

Most canoeists stay to established canoe routes,
portages and campsites. I do too, mostly. But I also
like to take off overland by compass, up and down,
across swamps and bogs, wherever. I've found some
fantastic vistas, game trails like highways, lush wild
flower and moss gardens, and some whopping big
trees.

AFTERWORD

Old Doc Log and I are very fortunate. That's an understatement. We are the luckiest two individuals in the world.

Because of the nature of our work, we *have* to visit the most beautiful places in the United States and Canada, I to record that beauty on film and in words, and Doc, well, he's got to be there when patients come to his couch.